YOUTUBE OPTIMIZATION – THE COMPLETE GUIDE

BY

TOM MARTIN

A huge thank you to Lisa and Sara my editors, without which this book would read like it was written by an algorithm, and to Luke and Fatma for making it look the part too.

Also a big hat tip to Chris, Chris, Tom and Caleb for pushing me over the line to get this published.

For Claire and the boys.

Every word I write and video I make is for you. Love you.

BONUS MATERIAL

n this book will be a great amount of actionable advice for you to digest and then execute on. However, it will be useless if you do not mplement what you learn after reading. With that in mind I have created a whole host of downloadable resources and videos that will help you to put all of these tips into practice.

This material includes:

✔ Click by click technical guides

✔ Video walkthroughs

✔ Downloadable worksheets and checklists

✔ Design templates

✔ Links to further resources and tools that I use every day on YouTube

To access all of the bonus material, free of charge simply visit: *www.FAQTube.tv/bonus*

CONTENTS

INTRODUCTION

Is content king on YouTube?

This is a point that has been debated since the first ever video was published on YouTube ten years ago (co-founder Jawed Karim's *Me A The Zoo)*. In recent years, however, the debate has been easy to quash with the use of two short but powerful words:

Watch Time

Watch Time is YouTube's single biggest ranking factor, and plays a huge part in saying what videos get surfaced to viewers in Search, the Suggested Video sidebar, the Home Page and other Browse Features.

But we should rewind a little first.

In the early days of YouTube, the promotion of a video and the ranking of a video in Search results was largely determined by view count. If a video gained good views initially, YouTube would see this as a sign that the video was valuable; YouTube would promote it, it would get more views - leading to more promotion. And so this virtuous circle went on.

However this system became too easy to game and people would inflate their view counts with paid views and bots (and by hitting the refresh button until their fingers bled) in order to get "organic" promotion from YouTube.

So back in 2012 YouTube made a switch to make Watch Time the heaviest weighted factor in its algorithm, the theory being that if people were watching lots of minutes of a video - and a high percentage of that video - then it must be good.

And YouTube want to promote good video (or video that gets watched) because it wants users to keep coming back again and again and watch more and more, because more views mean more ads served.

So, in theory, the best videos are the ones that are getting watched for the most time and for a high percentage of their duration and will rise to the top. They will automatically be pushed to people's Home Page and to the Suggested Videos sidebar, and rank higher in the Search Results.

Well that is the theory, but is that the reality?

In my opinion that is **a big fat NO.**

Disagree? Ok, let me ask you a question.

Ever look in the Search Results on YouTube to see where you are showing up?

Even if you are a YouTube Ninja, unfortunately you are not always going to take top spot.

And I know you have had the experience of clicking on someone that ranks above you and thinking... *This video sucks! How dare they place this above my latest masterpiece?*

Do not take it personally.

YouTube does not watch your video, so it uses a number of factors to make its ranking decisions: Watch Time, Tags, Engagement, Shares, Titles, Descriptions - to name just a few.

YouTube does not see how much effort you put into the video, how awesome it looks or how entertaining or useful it is.

You have to tell it.

That is **your** job.

This is YouTube Optimization and giving YouTube a nudge in the right direction, is really what it is all about.

Watch Time is a HUGE component in YouTube's algorithm and so the quality of your videos and the value they deliver should be at the front of your mind at all times.

What optimization is NOT is a silver bullet that can magically get views for bad videos.

Optimizing your videos will give them the best chance of success and allow them to reach their potential (and maximum audience).

Think of optimization as **a multiplier of quality**.

If we rank both quality and optimization on a scale of 1-10 (10 being most awesome) then a video with the highest quality, optimized to the fullest will be:

Quality **10 x** Optimization **10 = 100%** of potential success

But then consider a good video that is not well optimized:

Quality **10 x** Optimization **2 = 20%** potential success

That is the same exact video but now reaching only 20% of its potential because a few optimization steps were overlooked.

Now let us take another video on the same subject. It is a cool video but not as good as the first example, but it is well optimized:

Quality **7 x** Optimization **8 = 56%** potential success

I know this is oversimplified but it illustrates the reality that videos of an objectively lower standard can outperform and outrank better content simply because the uploader took the steps to optimize it for the platform.

It may not be fair but you can quote me on it:

"An average video with great metadata will always outperform a great video with average metadata."

The beauty of optimization is that once you have laid down the foundations and can understand the basic concepts it can be built into your production and publishing workflows so that you do not even notice you are doing it.

Another bonus is that it is never too late to take steps to optimize older videos.

I have seen huge spikes in views for videos that have sat collecting dust for years because of a small change to a Title or Thumbnail.

So how do we ensure that our quality video is reaching its full potential?

How do we ensure we are activating all of those important multipliers?

This is exactly why I have written this book, to ensure that you give your videos the best possible chance of being seen by your target audience and by the amount of people they deserve.

In the following chapters I have pulled together all of the optimization strategies needed for you to create the most platform-friendly YouTube videos possible. You just need to take action and implement them.

Although applying just one or two of these strategies will almost certainly have a positive effect, you should build all of them (or as many as possible) into your YouTube Channel management processes so that every video you publish achieves its full potential.

****

CHAPTER 1 – WATCH TIME

There are a number of important ranking factors that YouTube considers when surfacing your videos.

Watch Time is the mother of them all.

In the first days of the platform, a large amount of views of a video early on was a signal of success to YouTube and in turn it would promote it further. However it became too easy to artificially inflate a view count and game the YouTube algorithm.

As a result, YouTube changed its algorithm to reward videos that were actually being watched and not just being clicked on. This is much harder to game.

This "Audience Retention" is now incredibly important. Making sure that your videos get watched - and watched all the way through - is key. In fact it is *the* number one ranking factor affecting your video and the success of the other videos on your Channel.

If your videos are not getting watched you will not only hurt the chances of that video being discovered but also the discoverability of other videos on your Channel as YouTube deems you a less valuable source over all. With Watch Time so important you need to be thinking about it when creating videos and optimizing them for the platform.

Here is my guide to getting the best possible Watch Time rates.

Seven tips to increase YouTube Watch Time

1. Make epic content

I am not a great believer in the idea that content is king but for Watch Time it reigns supreme.

You can optimize until the cows come home but if someone arrives at your video only to find that it sucks, they are not going to stick around.

Make epic content that delivers value to the viewer and there is no way they will click away. A great viewing experience means they are also more likely to watch again, and - better yet - to share (another big ranking factor).

The videos do not have to be epic in production or production values either; they just need to reward the viewers in a way that goes above and beyond your competition.

Whatever categories your videos sit in ask yourself:

◆ *How can I blow people's minds with my usefulness?*

◆ *How can I change someone's life?*

◆ *How can I teach someone something that they never knew before?*

◆ *What is it about my next video that will make it impossible NOT to share?*

YouTube is full of average videos that never get watched so what can you make that will stand out from the crowd?

2. Have an optimized start

A video that starts with lots of waffle is **not** going to get watched. Attention spans just do not allow it.

Whether that is excessive branding, long-winded introductions or content that is irrelevant to the main subject, it needs to be cut.

Not only is it unnecessary, but if your viewers are clicking away early or this is going to hurt your Watch Time and your standing in YouTube's algorithm.

So how do you ensure your videos get off to the best start possible?

The first thing you can do to optimize the start of your video can be done before the video even begins.

Before someone has ever clicked on your video they use the Thumbnail and Title together to paint a picture in their heads of what to expect. Take any guesswork out of this for the viewer by using the Thumbnail and Title together to not only sell the video but to tee it up.

By doing this you have set up the story before it even begins, removing the need for any kind of introduction.

Here is a fine example of this from the PBS Idea Channel.

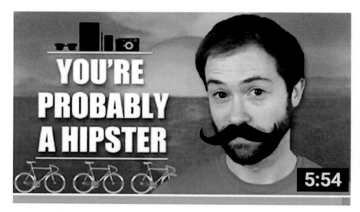

Are You A Hipster? | Idea Channel | PBS Digital Studios

YouTube.com/pbsideachannel

Here are three ways to ensure that once the video starts it does not get stopped:

◆ GET STRAIGHT TO THE POINT – if you have posed a question, answer it straight away, not three minutes into the video

◆ Move any branding from the start of the video to the end if it is longer than a few seconds. You may be impressed by your beautiful title sequence but for most people it is off-putting

◆ Keep greetings and intros short and simple but maintain your Channel's tone of voice. Personality and authenticity is very important on YouTube, so keep that in, just keep it quick

Think your video intros are pretty tight? Why not put it to the test?

The Wadsworth Constant. Ever heard of it? Thought not.

Well it is a theory that says that the first 30% of any YouTube video can be lost and the video will still make sense.

It originated on Reddit where someone realised how many videos on YouTube spent way too long on introductions and so The Wadsworth Constant was born.

You should try it. It is a real eye-opener.

There used to be a hack built into YouTube to test this but now you have to do things a little more manually, but here is how you do it:

As your video starts hit the number "3" key and the video will skip 30% in.

If your video still makes sense after this skip then it is time to get wieldy with the axe on your next video intro.

3. Keep it focused

A lot of people ask me what the perfect length of a YouTube video is. My answer is always:

A YouTube video should be as long as it is interesting and not a second longer.

It could be one minute, it could be half an hour, as long as it remains on-topic and gives the audience what they came for. All that matters is that people are staying tuned.

Stay focused and cut out anything that is not necessary for your video to work. Start to go off on a tangent and you have lost a big chunk of your audience.

Recently the waters have been muddied by the introduction of YouTube's subscription service called YouTube Red because this pays out based on the amount of monetized minutes watched.

You should not try to inflate the length of your videos in order to gain incremental revenue from YouTube Red unless you are certain this will not hurt your Audience Retention rates.

As with anything on YouTube, experiment, track the changes in YouTube Analytics and in this case, see how your Watch Time is affected.

For a free guide with a downloadable worksheet for benchmarking your YouTube Analytics please visit *www.FAQTube.tv/bonus*

4. Do not telegraph your ending

If the tone of your voice and content start to change as you wrap up your video, it is a clear indication to the audience that the video is over and people will click away.

Anything that is not essential viewing on YouTube does not get viewed.

Now that Autoplay has been introduced at the end of videos it is a crime to let this happen. I say this because if you are optimizing as much as possible it should almost always be your video lined up to play next, and by losing the viewer at this point you are missing out on an almost *guaranteed* view.

Keep the tone and pace level all the way up until the end so that viewers do not click off for fear of missing out.

Check out this great example of an optimized ending:

YouTube.com/faqtubetv

And see it in action by visiting *www.FAQTube.tv/endscreens*

5. Use past performance as a guide (YouTube Analytics)

The way that viewers have reacted to your content in the past is a good indication of how they will react in the future, especially if you have a consistent content strategy.

YouTube Analytics is a powerful tool and can be super helpful in the fight to keep Audience Retention high.

For Watch Time the best metric to track is Audience Retention.

The Channel average is a good indication of success but if you are adapting as you go the most recent videos are more relevant for this exercise. Look at your last six to ten videos and see where the audience starts to drop off.

Go to the videos in question and hit **Analytics > Audience Retention**.

Here is an example from one of my older videos:

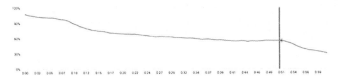

The dip (where the red line is) is where I am seeing the biggest drop off in Audience Retention for my video. The time corresponds with where I started to sign off, so in future videos I corrected this and have seen less drop-off towards the end of my videos.

You can check out my latest videos at *www.YouTube.com/faqtubetv*.

Check your analytics and see where the drop-offs occur and what they correspond to.

Most likely it will be:

◆ Where you start to wrap up (see point 4)

◆ Where you ask people to click to another video

◆ When you have answered the question the video sets out to answer or delivers on its "hook" (see chapter 3)

◆ Where you start to go off-topic or lose focus

Another cool thing to check while you are in Analytics is how your Audience Retention rates compare to the YouTube average. Just hit the **Relative Audience Retention** box to compare the two.

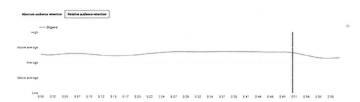

6. Tease something that is coming up

This can be an early visual flash of something that will be coming up later in the video or a verbal tease designed to keep people watching until the end of the video.

Some people swear by this and some people (myself included) think this can contradict point 2 and will mean that your introduction may be unnecessarily long.

The idea is that you start the video by teasing something that is coming up at the end of the video as an incentive to stick around.

I think for this to work you need to have a highly engaged audience that want to hear all you have to say in the lead-up to the pay-off and not viewers who are dropping by for a quick answer to a question.

As with all things I would suggest you experiment and see how it affects your Audience Retention rates.

The stats do not lie.

7. Do not use misleading metadata

It can be very tempting to try a few tricks and hacks to show up in more Search Results and Suggested Videos but attempts to manipulate YouTube's algorithm with unrelated metadata is usually a one-way ticket to failure.

Not only are you in breach of YouTube's Community Guidelines (read Terms Of Service), you can also hurt your SEO.

How?

Well, when viewers find your video and do not get what they want because it was misrepresented by your metadata then they are likely to click away - and fast.

This will hurt your Audience Retention rates and damage your future rankings.

Place *quality* views over the *quantity of* views and the traffic will follow as well as the algorithmic boost. This is the goal of any YouTube Channel manager.

Create content with your audience (and Audience Retention rates) in mind and you are much more likely to make content that people just cannot click away from.

You will then start to see the benefit to your individual videos and ultimately, your YouTube Channel as a whole.

Closely related to Watch Time is Session Time, which we will look at next.

****

CHAPTER 2 - SESSION TIME

Session Time optimization is the hardest of all my recommendations to measure but remains one of the most important.

Like Watch Time, Session Time affects the ranking and surfacing of individual videos and on a Channel-wide level, so needs to be taken very seriously.

This is very rarely spoken about but in this chapter I have outlined some steps that will have you keeping Session Times in the forefront of your YouTube strategy.

As far as ranking factors on YouTube go, Session Time is up there with the big boys.

How come?

Well, YouTube do not have to do much to get people onto its platform - people are linking to it and sharing videos left right and centre - but to make real money they need users to stay around and watch *more* videos.

This means that if your videos lead to longer sessions for YouTube users, your video will be rewarded as the "gateway" video to a long session, **even if they are not watching your videos.**

Unlike some other optimization tactics this is not always in your direct control but there are definitely things that you can do to optimize for longer Session Times.

The reward?

Better Search Rankings and more of your videos being surfaced in the Suggested Videos sidebar.

Follow these steps to help you achieve this...

Six steps to generate longer YouTube Session Times

1. Optimized SEO

If viewers are going to go on and watch a long list of other videos after your "gateway" video, then they may as well be yours, right?

Easier said than done, I know.

But if your Channel and videos are optimized for SEO as much as possible you will see the amount of Suggested Videos belonging to you start to dominate that sidebar.

This also has the advantage in that the more Suggested Videos that belong to you, the less chance there is of users being recommended a lower quality video that may cause them to end a session.

Session Time and Watch Time make up a huge amount of SEO but we will tackle the other factors such as Metadata and engagement in later chapters.

2. Playlists

In terms of having a direct influence over Session Times I think that Playlists may be the most effective method.

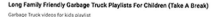
Long Family Friendly Garbage Truck Playlists For Children (Take A Break)

Garbage Truck videos for kids playlist

GARBAGE TRUCK Videos For ... Children I 45 MINUTES of Toys Garbage Trucks Rule 208,342 views • 1 year ago

Garbage Truck Videos For ... Children, Diggers, Excavator Garbage Trucks Rule 9,497 views • 1 year ago

Garbage Truck Videos For Children I Tons Of Fun! Let's Pla... Garbage Trucks Rule 263,113 views • 11 months ago

GARBAGE TRUCK VIDEOS For ... Children I Playing With BRUDER Garbage Trucks Rule 38,643 views • 11 months ago

YouTube.com/garbagetrucksrule

I have always been a huge fan of Playlists and have preached their benefits to everyone that I have worked on a YouTube Channel with.

he benefits of Playlists have not always been tangible but since the ntroduction of Playlist Analytics, people can see directly what a Playlist an do for their Channel.

Jsing Playlists can greatly increase a viewer's Session Time because naturally people are watching a number of videos in a row without eaving YouTube. Even if not all the videos in the Playlist are yours, you vill still be rewarded for the long session.

t is for this reason that my number one tip for Playlists is that the first video should always be your own, even if you are curating other people's content. This way you increase your chances of being that gateway to a onger session.

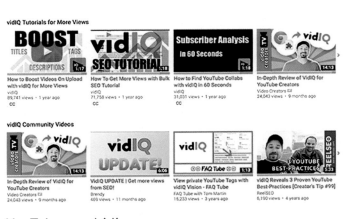

YouTube.com/vidiq

itill need convincing that Playlists are worth the small amount of time and effort they take to create? Here are another five solid gold reasons why I think every video you create should go into a Playlist:

. Association of Videos

Anything that increases the association between your videos is going to be a huge SEO boost.

f they are viewed together regularly in Playlists, YouTube is going to iee the relationship between the two and is more likely to suggest

the same journey in Suggested Videos, even when viewed outside o
Playlist mode.

II. Activation of older content

If you have a large number of videos on your Channel it is easy for the
older ones to stop getting views. This starts a vicious cycle as they get
less promotion and then even fewer views going forward.

Use the popularity of newer videos to highlight older videos by putting
them in Playlists together, grouping them by themes or topics.

For example, if I have a new review video of the latest season of *Better
Call Saul*, I would create a Playlist that includes my reviews of previous
seasons that otherwise would not be resurfaced.

III. They are embeddable

I think that this feature is incredibly useful, especially if you already
have a strong outreach strategy.

Being able to embed a Playlist means that if a blog is interested in a
number of your videos they can embed them all in a Playlist without

aving to embed them separately. This cuts down the space on page nd also the time and effort required on their part.

'ou should also be embedding Playlists on your own blog or website vhere you can.

f you don't have one, why not?

V. They are great for SEO

part from the Session Time benefit to the SEO of your Channel, 'laylists can also be useful in targeting new Keywords that the original 'ideos do not.

f a trending topic is gathering pace why not put together a Playlist, naking sure to include the trending Keywords in your Playlist lescription and Title.

V. Increased footprint on the platform

he more videos you have on the platform the more chances there are f someone finding you. This can be amplified with very little effort by reating Playlists.

'laylists can be found in Search and this increases the likelihood of omeone discovering your Channel without having to create any extra 'ideos. I think I have made my point that Playlists on YouTube deliver a ot of benefits for very little effort, so l will move on to the next strategy use to increase session time.

3. End Screen calls to action

(eep End Screens (or end boards) short and sweet and, most importantly, elevant to the video that has just been viewed.

iive them just a few choices to prevent indecision and inaction and do t in the following formats, with #1 being the most effective and going n order from there:

I. A human, in vision, giving a verbal call to action and physically pointing where to click

II. A human in-vision giving a verbal call to action

III. Voiceover telling people where to click

IV. Burned in graphical call to action

At the time of writing, YouTube have just released a new End Screen feature that allows you to create a bespoke End Screen with clickable widgets that work on mobile.

The new feature lets you seamlessly give clickable calls to action in vision as well as the option of professional and clickable graphical calls to action.

Best Budget Vlogging Set Up for Starting a
Business Vlog on YouTube

YouTube.com/simplebusinessvideo

I would recommend finishing all of your videos by creating your End Screens with this new tool for the best possible click through rates.

Check out the bonus section to watch my video on how to use this feature and how to get the most out of them - *www.FAQTube.tv/bonus*

4. Link out with caution

YouTube is part of Google and Google *loves* links.

External links to relevant sites tell Google that you are trying to give the user all they need to solve their problem. It is because of this that I advise placing external links in your descriptions.

However, any link that takes a viewer off-platform is a huge risk to end that current session, so use with caution.

Link only to your own properties if it helps your wider business and to external parties if it is likely to be detrimental to your viewers if excluded.

Of course you can be as liberal as you like with internal YouTube links and in fact it will help your ranking to promote other people's content.

The biggest **bonus tip** I can give on using links is that whenever you link to one of your own videos make sure you link to it in "Playlist Mode."

To do this, navigate to the Playlist that the video in question sits in, click on that particular video and then copy and paste the URL that now includes the Playlist information.

This means that when a viewer clicks on it now they are smack bang in the middle of the Playlist and therefore likely to watch more of your videos and increase the Session Time.

5. Promote discussion

The amount of comments and engagement your video gets will have an effect (even if only small) on the ranking and surfacing of your videos across the platform. This is because YouTube sees that your videos are either gaining lots of Likes or Shares, or that it is inspiring discussion in the comments and so is a great video or Channel to be sending viewer to.

Add to this the fact that time spent on the Watch Page of your video while in discussion increases viewers' Session Time and it makes sense to switch out some of those subscribe calls to action for some prompt to comment.

You can also encourage discussion in the comments by posing question to your audience, as you may have noticed people in YouTube comment are not shy in sharing their opinions.

What kind of discussion would it be if you were not involved?

You can use YouTube's new Pinned Comment feature to make sure you question and thread stay at the top of the comments:

Make sure to jump in and join the discussion. This has the benefit o increasing the comment count but as viewers can see you are responding to comments they are more likely to get involved.

Another new feature you can use to encourage increased comments i to reward your community members with a Creator Heart for a commen you like or appreciate. The Heart is public and so will likely encourage not only more comments but better quality comments as they strive to earn a Heart from you too.

I would suggest that you use these sparingly though so that they maintain their perceived value.

Another really powerful way to promote comments is to screenshot and shout out commenters in later videos. This has been used to great effect by the likes of Fine Brothers Entertainment and Screen Junkies, and some Channels such as the official Doctor Who channel have even based entire formats on them –

Throwback Thursday - Doctor Who -
#ThrowbackThursday

YouTube.com/doctorwho

Now, you may not have to go as far as this but if you are a small enough Channel, have lots of time or a team to help, try responding to as many comments as possible. This way you will grow a community as well as improve your video SEO.

6. Increase session starts

The more times yours can be the first video that people visit on their YouTube journey, the more you will be rewarded as the gateway to a long session.

The most obvious way to do this is to ensure that your Subscribers have their notifications turned on. That may not be easy, depending on your audience and style of content, but try and remind them from time to time in your calls to action to hit the Notification Bell after subscribing.

How To Get Notifications From Your Favourite YouTubers

YouTube.com/davidwalshonline

To get more people to start more sessions you will need to leverage as many techniques as you can off platform in order to get them onto YouTube.

These include growing your Social Media presence, joining online communities and forums, paid traffic (if you have the budget and know-how) and - my top tip - growing an email list that you own and can send your own notifications to.

With all of the notifications we receive across our devices, email seems to be one of the few that people still take notice of.

The tracking of Session Time is nigh on impossible and so is often overlooked, but the six steps outlined above are all easy to implement and are practices that you should already be carrying out.

Ultimately, if you scratch YouTube's back by increasing Session Time, it will scratch yours by making it easier for people to find your videos. Everyone wins.

The next three recommendations are what I like to call **The Three T's**. These are three types of optimization that can get you some quick wins but are also a good place to start for a long-term optimization strategy.

A quick note before we proceed though. Although I have yet to witness it, it is possible that making a change to a video's Title, Tags or other Metadata could have a negative effect on a video going forward. If you have a video that is performing well for you and you are generally risk averse you may want to err on the side of caution and leave that particular video as it is.

****

CHAPTER 3 – YOUTUBE TITLES

There is a reason that sites like BuzzFeed and Mail Online have such amazing traffic numbers and, guess what, it is not because of their world class content (confession - BuzzFeed is a guilty pleasure of mine)

It is their headlines.

The YouTube equivalent of this is a Title. This is the feature that really sells your video to viewers, and, make no mistake, you are now a sales person - whether you like it or not.

Make it sexy, make it pique curiosity and make it irresistible for browsers not to click on.

Titles are doubly important because they also have enormous SEO value.

A good video Title can be a hook, a promise or a tease and in this chapter I will show you the fundamentals of creating YouTube Titles to outrank and outshine your competition.

6-pack Abs: Yoga Style! With Fightmaster Yoga

YouTube.com/fightmasteryoga

Along with the Thumbnail, your video's Title may be the only part of your video that ever gets seen by the public.

How good those two things are will determine if they convert someone from a browser to a viewer.

You will only have a few seconds to attract a browser and the Title and Thumbnail should work together to sell him or her a video that is irresistible.

They should let the viewer know exactly what to expect when they click, allowing you to get straight into the meat and potatoes of your video for an optimized start.

How to Make Buffalo Cauliflower Bites | Hilah Cooking

YouTube.com/hilahcooking

There is no perfect formula for optimal Titles but there are best practices and a few extra tweaks that I have picked up as a Certified YouTube Channel Manager, and I want to share them with you.

The fundamentals of YouTube Titles

Length

The length of a video Title is not really important and you will not be penalised for using up your character allowance.

What *will* hurt is if you do not frontload the Title with the most interesting aspect of the video, or the "Hook."

When YouTube was more of a visually static platform it was widely known that the Hook had to be given in the first 40 characters or it would be cut off in Search results and Suggested Videos.

Luckily the platform is more responsive and forgiving now, but the importance of hooking your viewer with the start of the Title remains.

Keeping it succinct is essential.

Talk To Me

YouTube.com/dreupt

One tip that I use is to try and remove "stop" words where possible – words like "*the*", "*and*" and, "*a*". These words are useless to search engines and you can get your message across without them.

f your Title does not flow after removing them, try using shortened versions like "&" instead of "and", or "w/" instead of "with".

You can use any separators that you like between sections of a Title, as search engines will ignore them.

f you are in a more fun niche, why not use some of the more eye-catching buttons on the keyboard instead of hyphens to help draw the eye? What about an emoji?

YouTube.com/tubebuddy

Structure

Here is the YouTube Title structure I would advise you to use, whatever your content:

Hook – Explainer – Show Information – Channel Information

Here is a hypothetical example of a clip taken from *Seinfeld*, my favourite TV show *ever*.

No Soup For You! – Elaine Vs. Soup Nazi – Seinfeld – Seinfeld On Demand

As mentioned above the Hook is what will be of interest to most people and allow you the most creative flair.

Keep it short and punchy and, most importantly, keep it at the front.

It is the part of the Title that is most likely to get it clicked and should also include the Keywords you are aiming to rank for.

Build Massive Shoulders Fast (Gym Workout)

YouTube.com/sixpackfactoryabs

The Explainer is like a tagline, or what comes after the colon in the title of a bad movie.

Foundations Of Yoga - Camel Pose - Ustrasana

YouTube.com/yogawithadriene

t allows you to give a little more detail and slip in a few more Keywords hat will be of interest to the viewer or searcher. This may not be ecessary for all videos.

he Show and Channel information are more for the search engines han the human eye but still work to give viewers a point of reference, specially if you have an episodic structure (Part 1, Part 2 etc.).

Facing The Hound - The Hounds of Baskerville - Sherlock - BBC

YouTube.com/sherlock221b

hese are also useful as Keywords; consistent use of them in your Titles also in your Tags and Descriptions) will create a stronger association between your videos.

his means you are more likely to turn up in your own Suggested Videos ection and this is where you will really start to see an uplift in views.

)o not get too bogged down in the terminology I have used. Stick to t as closely or as loosely as fits your Channel but do implement the undamentals.

Here is another example I have created for an imaginary retro gaming Channel:

Epic Finish Him | Let's Play Mortal Kombat Pt. 5 | Coin-Op Palace

Like anything on YouTube, you will get out of it what you put in.

Give as much thought to the Title as you do to filming or editing. Marketing is just as important (if not more so) than your content.

You may have a great video but who will click on it if it does not have an appealing Title?

I would take that sentiment even further and say:

"If you cannot think of a good Title for your YouTube video do not make the video."

Go back through your older videos too and optimize the Titles using the standards above and you should notice an improvement.

This is a quick win and results can be dramatic.

YouTube Optimization can definitely be considered both an art and a science and nowhere is that more obvious than with your YouTube Titles.

Having just covered the fundamentals (the science) of Titles, it is time to look at the art.

Seven YouTube Title types that convert

This is the part where you put on your Mad Men style hat and get into creative copywriting mode.

It is time to sell.

As I said in the previous section, the most important part of your Title is the Hook. This is the sexy, descriptive part that has the biggest impact on a browser or searcher. These are the words viewers use to make a split second decision – Is your video worth my time?

There are a number of ways to make your Hook as clickable as possible and here are just some of the go-to formats that I use and that I *know* attract viewers.

1. *How To*

This is the king of the evergreen Title.

People use this term to search for videos all the time on both YouTube and Google, so if you are making an instructional video, including "How To" at the start will definitely help increase those long tail views.

How To Brush Your Hair....
Correctly? | Ultimate Guide To...

YouTube.com/realmenrealstyle

2. Vs.

There is nothing people like more in life than a good ol' fashioned showdown.

Whether it is two wild animals, two pop divas (what is the difference, right?) or two models of mobile phone, adding these two letters to a Title gives it a fighting chance of success.

Canon 80D vs. 70D (Is It Worth The Upgrade?)

YouTube.com/calebwojcik

3. The Remarkable ("Epic" "Awesome" "Incredible")

This one should be used sparingly to maintain its impact but it can be a powerful weapon to bring out for the right video.

In his book "*Contagious: Why Things Catch On*," Jonah Berger says that it is the appeal of the remarkable that can help to send things viral, and there is no coincidence that many a viral hit starts with a sensationalist adjective.

Heartbreaking! Ultimate Penguin Sacrifice - Life in the Freezer -...

YouTube.com/bbcearth

4. Trend Friendly

Where relevant, you should find what is trending on YouTube and use trends to shape your content.

By using Keywords of topics that are trending you leverage the Search Traffic that those terms are already receiving to get more views.

However, you need to make sure that when you leverage these trending terms you do not alienate your Subscribers and that Keywords are not crowbarred in too clumsily.

Trends on YouTube can be fleeting so you need to know where to look in order to stay ahead of the curve. For a list of the most up to date places to find what is trending on YouTube make sure to check out the bonus material for this book at *www.FAQTube.tv/bonus*.

Once you know what trend you are trying to ride the wave of, make sure that the trending term is front and centre in the Title (and also present in your Tags and Description).

Types of trend-friendly video can be an explainer, parody or reaction video, all of which can get huge amounts of views in the wake of a trend.

Pen Pineapple Apple Pen ⚡🍍🍎 ⚡ PPAP

YouTube.com/chadwildclay

5. Question

Almost nothing piques the interest and curiosity of the more intellectually leaning YouTube viewer than an unanswered question.

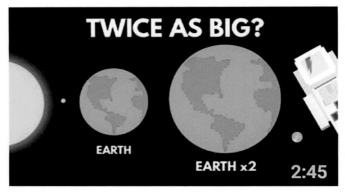

What If The Earth Were Twice As Big?

YouTube.com/lifenoggin

This is an age-old copywriting technique that has passed the test of ime and continues to help numerous Channels to get millions of views.

Remember, though, if you are going to raise a question you damn well better answer it, or you are going to have a very unhappy audience.

5. Functional but SEO friendly

Short but sweet. Simple yet effective.

These Titles do not mess around, get straight to the point and are Keyword rich. They do not waste space with superlatives and minimize stop words, resulting in higher Search rankings.

RODE VideoMic Me | Test and Review

YouTube.com/simpleaudiotips

For maximum effect on these types of video I would suggest using a Keyword research tool to find out exactly what people are searching for and how they are phrasing it.

I personally recommend a tool called Vid IQ (see bonus section for more details - *www.FAQTube.tv/bonus*), which also gives you an indication of whether a term is trending up or is waning in popularity.

7. Lists

How could I complete this list without including the List Video?

You may be sick to death of being sent BuzzFeed "listicles" but YouTube is still lapping them up.

Tell the audience what they are getting and how many and no doubt you will not only get views but people sticking around to see what is number one.

Top 10 Bruce Lee Moments

YouTube.com/WatchMojo

You do not have to use top tens and using seemingly random numbers can actually help increase curiosity. Take a look at a magazine rack next time you are passing and see this in action.

Here I have outlined a powerful list of potential Title formats, although some of these formats will not work for your niche.

Let us take a look at a hypothetical example of a video explaining how to clean your false teeth:

Epic denture cleaning tutorial (Remarkable)

This may not be suitable for an oral hygiene Channel, but they would be able to utilise a few of the formats:

How to sterilise dentures for free (How To)

7 free denture cleaning tips (List)

Why do dentures get smelly? (Question)

The beautiful thing about Titles is that you can change them and experiment.

Make sure you are tracking changes in YouTube Analytics so you can see how effective the changes were and what *your* audience react well to.

Now for the second of the *Three T's,* YouTube Tags.

****

CHAPTER 4 - TAGS

These little beauties are the main weapon for your "on-page" Video SEO and work closely with your Titles and Descriptions.

These should be Keyword-rich, consistent, and trend-friendly. By taking the ten steps in the next section you will be able to do this across all of your videos.

With optimal Tags in place not only will your individual videos rank higher in Search and be surfaced more in Suggested Videos but you will create a relationship between your videos that leads to longer Session Times where people watch a number of your videos.

There are many myths and lots of bad advice floating out there on the Internet regarding Tags, but if you follow my ten-step guide you will be safe in the knowledge that you are creating Tags in a way that is optimized for YouTube's algorithm.

Steps to create optimal Tags for YouTube videos

1. Create Upload Default Tags

YouTube's Creator Academy suggests that you should "*include a mix of video-specific and more general (but still relevant) Tags.*" It is these Default Tags that take care of the "*more general*" part of that recommendation.

Default Tags are present on the Basic Info tab of a video's Info & Settings page and are auto-populated for all new uploads, meaning that you do not have to keep adding Tags that you use regularly.

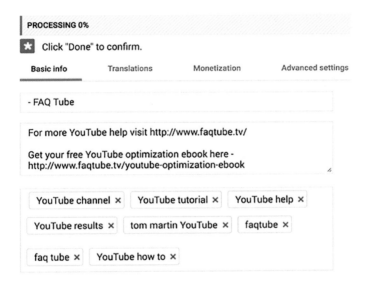

There is a reason for using Default Tags beyond convenience, and that is that if consistent Tags are present in all videos on your Channel, it helps to create a relationship between your videos.

This relationship is invaluable to Creators as it means that more of your videos will be served in the Suggested Videos sidebar, which is a huge source of views.

For your Default Tags you want to include:

◆ **Channel Keywords** – Keywords that relate to your brand such a Channel name, tagline, talent names etc. and

◆ **Subject Keywords** – What topics do you cover? What categories What Keywords do you want your Channel to rank for?

I would suggest aiming for about six to ten Default Tags (see point 3 o this chapter for more on the ideal number of Tags).

As an example here are my Channel Default Tags again:

Upload Default Tags can be set by navigating to **Creator Studio > Channe > Upload Defaults** and need to be separated in quotation marks:

To watch a video walking you through the processes of setting these Defaults and for some bonus tips on getting these Default Tags righ first time (remember they will appear on every new video you upload) check out my guide in the bonus section - *www.FAQTube.tv/bonus*

2. Use video specific Tags

Now that you have Upload Default Tags in place you will see them or every new upload. You can place your video specific Tags after them in he Tags box, safe in the knowledge that Tag placement does not affect anking.

'ou want to use Tags that succinctly sum up the topic of your video and re not covered in your Upload Defaults.

"hese can be things like subjects covered, names mentioned, themes ooked at and formats used.

Check out my tags here for my video titled *"Live Video Available To All"* is an example:

VIDEO TAGS

YouTube channel   YouTube tutorial   YouTube help
YouTube results   tom martin YouTube   faqtube   faq tube
YouTube how to   mobile live stream   youtube live stream
youtube mobile live   go live on youtube   youtube live
how many subscribers to go live on youtube

"his is all about granular detail and helping YouTube to help others ind your videos by telling it what the video is about.

5. *Use as many Tags as necessary*

"here is no magic number for the amount of Tags you should use. Use is many as is necessary and do not try to keep them low or to add extra ones to fill the box.

Jse the amount of Tags needed to convey your major Keywords without becoming spammy. If this is eight Tags, fine. If you fill up the box, so be it.

Think about Tags like instant coffee – *stay with me here.*

'ou want to add enough water so that it is not too strong, but not so much water that it becomes diluted or weak.

So do not dilute your Tags by filling them up with junk and do not short change yourself by not including enough relevant Keywords.

Like many things on YouTube, it is an art and a science.

Ask yourself this question for each tag you add:

"If the person finds this video by searching for this Keyword will they b *disappointed by what they see?"*

If the answer is *Yes,* then you should not be including that Tag, a disappointed viewers will hurt your Watch Time when they click awa early on.

4. Do not use misleading Tags

I have seen numerous people advocating the use of popular Channe names and other misleading Keywords. The theory behind this is t create a false association between Channels in order to rank for popula but unrelated Keywords.

Do **NOT** do this.

In the short term you may see a boost in views but your Watch Time wil suffer when people click expecting one thing but receive somethin very different, only to leave after a few seconds.

Stay honest and keep a long-term view of your Channel's success, a you will achieve deeper engagement by delivering what you promis via accurate metadata.

It may be a slower route to the top of the Search rankings but it is legitimate and, more importantly, sustainable strategy.

5. Keyword research

This is such an important technique and is vital when tagging you videos. It is probably also the most underused weapon in the arsenal o a YouTube Channel manager.

expect Keyword research is overlooked because it is not easy and YouTube have made it harder by closing its Keyword Tool that used to be available to the public.

Keyword research techniques are complicated, involve a number of tools and are unfortunately beyond the scope of this book but if you check out the bonus section (*www.FAQTube.tv/bonus*) I have a guide here to get you started.

6. *Do not split up terms into separate Tags*

If you have a Keyword or Key Phrase that you want to rank for that contains multiple words, do not split them up.

For example, if you are trying to rank for "*Best BBQ Sauce Recipe*" I would include that as a single Tag.

What I would suggest for very important terms within Key Phrases however, is to spin them out into their own Tag.

For example, in my imaginary Sauce Recipe video I would definitely want to rank for the term "BBQ Sauce." As "Recipe" is also a general category I would probably include that too, if it were not already in my defaults:

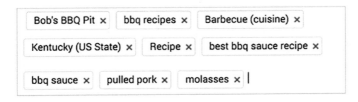

Use these "duplicate" Tags sparingly though, as you do not want to dilute your Tags.

7. *Forget misspellings and synonyms*

Do not waste valuable Tags by including misspellings of Keywords in an attempt to mop up rogue Search traffic.

Google powers YouTube's search engine. It uses the same convention as its flagship search engine so your videos will also be found b misspellings and synonyms. *It's clever like that.*

If you have the choice of two similar words but do not want to Tag then both, use a Google Trends search to see which word gets more Searcl traffic and is gaining more momentum and use that as a Tag.

Watch my video in the bonus section to see how to use Google Trend for YouTube Keyword research - *www.FAQTube.tv/bonus*.

8. Look at your competitor's Tags

Previously on YouTube the Tags for a video were displayed publicly or the Watch Page. This was very useful for smart Channel managers likt you and me.

But back in 2012, YouTube took the decision to make Tags private. Th reason for this was solid. There was lots of shady SEO going down.

People copied Tags wholesale from popular videos and added them tt videos that they were not relevant to. The copycats hoped that thei video would now show up in the Search results and Suggested Video of the original.

I think this move by YouTube makes perfect sense. I have alway advocated keeping squeaky clean and would never suggest trying tt game YouTube's algorithm.

However, I genuinely believe that you can learn from seeing othe people's Tags without plagiarizing (I will show you how shortly), whicl is why I use a free tool to view other people's Tags and why I recommenc you do the same.

The tool I am talking about is a free Google Chrome extension callec vidIQ (requires you to sign up for an account), which allows you to viev the Tags of all videos on YouTube, as well as a whole host of othe useful stats and insights.

You can get more information on the tool and download it directly at the following link: *www.FAQTube.tv/vidiqvision*

Once installed you have this amazing on-screen widget every time you play a video on YouTube that displays the video's Tags.

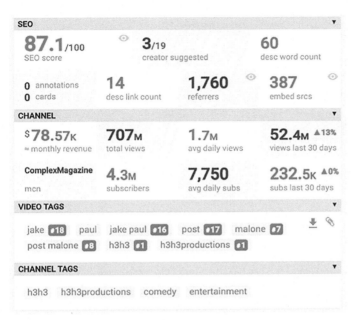

Get stuck in as soon as possible and see how others in your space (and outside of it) are tagging their videos and what terms they are targeting.

What Keywords are your competition (or similar Channels in your niche) utilising that you have overlooked? Add them to your Default Tags (where relevant) and retrospectively to videos that are already live.

You will notice that I said "where relevant" above. Do not just copy YouTube Tags wholesale.

As mentioned previously, every Tag that you use should be hyper-relevant to your video, as you do not want them to be diluted by Keywords that are not applicable.

Secondly, it is important to keep point 4 from this chapter in mind when using this technique.

You do not want to appear in irrelevant searches because people click on your video and leave early after not getting what they searched for. This leads to negative Audience Retention rates that hurt your videos chances of being recommended by the algorithm in the future.

Lastly, you should not copy Tags indiscriminately as it is not fair to the original poster. They worked on their Tags as much as they have on their video and, like any original creation, it should not be ripped off.

9. Refresh Tags for new trends

The great thing about YouTube is how you can adjust things even after they go live. Refreshing your Tags is a perfect example of this.

If you are keeping your eyes open for YouTube trends you may notice that one of your older videos is now relevant to a trending topic. Add Tags to the existing video that relate to the trending topic and hopefully it will be swept up in the Search traffic and Suggested Videos.

We have established that Tags do two things:

◆ Help videos to rank in Search for certain Keywords and

◆ Create relationships between two videos, leading to more views from Suggested Videos

Both of these are the bread and butter of a YouTube Channel manager.

Follow all of the above steps for new videos and revisit videos that you have already published to make sure they live up to the same standard and you should see an upward trend in your YouTube analytics.

Now to the last of the *Three T's...*

****

CHAPTER 5 – THE EXPANDED GUIDE TO YOUTUBE THUMBNAILS

A picture is worth a thousand words" as the old adage goes. They can be worth thousands of views too if you know how to choose or create optimal YouTube Thumbnails.

You can work tirelessly to get your videos to appear higher in Search results and be served as a Suggested Video, but if your Thumbnail is not easy on the eye then no one will click on it.

That said, the YouTube Creator Academy only dedicates a few column inches on the subject of Thumbnails and so I am going to expand on their advice and give a few extra tips that I use to make sure that my videos get clicked on.

Firstly, here are the YouTube Thumbnail size and specification details:

- Have a resolution of 1280×720 (with a minimum width of 640 pixels).

- Be uploaded in image formats such as JPG, .GIF, .BMP, or .PNG.

- Remain under the 2 MB limit.

- Try to use a 16:9 aspect ratio, as it is the most used in YouTube players and previews.

After all, *what is the point of creating a masterpiece if you can't use it?*

Now we have got the image specs covered, here are the General Guidelines that are given by YouTube as best practice.

I have expanded on each one to help you put these into action and achieve a better click through rate.

General Guidelines

1. Always upload custom Thumbnails with the video file

I have moved this to the top of the list as I think it is most obvious.

A custom image is almost always going to be a better choice than the auto-generated options that YouTube provide, not only because of image quality but also because of the importance of the next point...

2. Design Thumbnails that reinforce your videos' Titles – make sure that together they tell a cohesive story

What's in My Backpack? - College Info Geek

YouTube.com/thomasfrank

When a Thumbnail accurately portrays what is being said in the Title they work together and become more inviting for those people who would be interested in what you have to offer while weeding out the people who are not.

But I want as many views as possible on my videos.

Actually, you do not. Not short, incomplete views that hurt your Audience Retention rate.

Low Audience Retention rates hurt the likelihood of a singular video being surfaced by the algorithm. It also affects the surfacing of other videos in your Channel as a whole.

A strong combination of Title and Thumbnail will allow you to have an optimized start to your video because together they have already set up the premise of the video so there is no need for a long-winded introduction. This will greatly improve your Audience Retention stats.

3. When shooting a video, take shots that will make great Thumbnails

Crochet for Knitters - Granny Square Blanket

YouTube.com/verypinkknits

YouTube does not know the selling point of your video, so there is very little chance that it will give you an auto-generated option that will represent it well.

A well-timed screen grab can be extremely effective but will rarely have the impact of a specially shot image (or a sweet composition put together on Photoshop).

So when planning production, think of the Thumbnail in advance (like you should be doing with your Titles) and make sure you get a perfect still shot during production to create the Thumbnail you envisioned.

4. Make sure the Thumbnail is not overly sexually provocative

Top 10 Sexiest Music Videos

YouTube.com/WatchMojo

This will depend on your definition of *"overly"* but sex does sell. Sex gets clicked.

There is a reason those Fail compilations have millions of views.

Rule of thumb = You should be fine with some provocation as long as there are no nipples on show.

That is absolutely not a reason to include cleavage in your Thumbnail if your video is about remote control cars.

Moving swiftly on, here are the Visual Guidelines for Thumbnails, as set out by YouTube:

'isual Guidelines

. Clear, in-focus, hi-resolution (640px x 360px min., 16:9 aspect ratio)

'hese will be seen on screens of varying sizes and a high-resolution mage will mean they retain quality across all of them.

 16:9 ratio is a must, as any black bars look untidy and unprofessional.

▶ Bright, high-contrast

▶ Foreground stands out from background

}oth of these will mean a sharper image, which can be seen at smaller izes and will also catch the eye of viewers on very cluttered Search ›ages.

PURPLE SONG ♫| Learn Colors with Pancake Manor | Song for

YouTube.com/pancakemanor

These will also help you stand out against competition in the Suggested /ideos sidebar.

2. Looks great at both small and large sizes

This is *extremely* important.

It is all well and good if your Thumbnail looks like a Van Gogh on giant screen but how many people will actually see it that way?

More and more views now come from mobile and tablet (at least 50% according to YouTube's last update) and so your images need to be jus as effective on a much smaller scale. Make sure you zoom out from you image to check this before you upload.

It is for this reason that I advise against using excessive text in Thumbnail unless absolutely necessary. Videos are rarely seen withou their Title right next to them and it can be a waste of space to replicat your Title on the Thumbnail. This is especially detrimental when tha Thumbnail is seen on Mobile.

However for some types of content including Vlogs and How To video many Thumbnails would be lacklustre without the text.

You can also be clever and use text that compliments the Title, an works in tandem with it rather than just repeating it.

Why Following Your Passion Is BAD ADVICE!

YouTube.com/GideonShalwick

3. Close-ups of faces

I'm not sure for the exact theory behind this tip but no doubt it is rooted in Psychology.

If you are going to show a face in a Thumbnail, the mouth should be open and you should be able to see the whites of the person's eyes.

A person's eyes are very linked to trust so having them visible is important and the open mouth evokes action and conversation.

Airshou 0.6.1 is Back For Free Without Jailbreak! How to Recor...

YouTube.com/vgjfelix

4. Visually compelling imagery

This would go towards reinforcing my previous point and choosing the right image is key.

Go for something action-based or something out of the ordinary. Differentiate yourself from the competition.

Driving into the Unknown: Mongol Rally Adventure Documentary –

YouTube.com/returnoftheyak

Can your Thumbnail tell a story or paint a picture even without the Title? If so, you are doing a god job.

5. Well-framed, good composition

A well-composed image makes it more likely to catch the eye. It also gives a clue to the quality of the video.

7 Ways to Turn Your Bathroom Into a SPA!

YouTube.com/cleanmyspace

f it is clear you have put more time and effort into producing your nage than the competition, it is likely you have done the same for your ideo.

)o not let a sloppy Thumbnail convey a bad impression of your videos. 'ut in the effort and you will reap the rewards by converting more rowsers into viewers.

i. *Accurately represents the content*

ll roads lead back here.

t the risk of repeating myself, targeting views just to bolster your view ount will not help you in the long term.

udience Retention and Watch Time are the holy grail of a YouTube channel and enticing people with false advertising is a way to lose ;ubscribers, not gain them.

Make it sensationalist, make it sexy, make it stand out, but make sure 'ou can deliver on it.

World's Best Choux with chef Joakim Prat | Maitre Choux,...

YouTube.com/oramatvofficial

It is important to remember too that YouTube does not take kindly to misleading Thumbnails and it remains one of the few reasons that someone can flag your video or Channel to YouTube.

Apart from the above points that YouTube initially recommend, I think there are a few fundamentals that have been overlooked and you need to integrate them into your processes.

Three bonus tips for better YouTube Thumbnails

1. Consistency

Like all of your branding on YouTube, keeping a consistent style across your Thumbnails will help with recognition and association. This recognition factor can be invaluable in setting your videos apart in search results and Suggested Videos.

Some people like to put their Channel logo on their Thumbnails, but I think it is overkill and can make a Thumbnail a bit too busy, especially on mobile.

If you do want to brand your Thumbnails, do not do it at the expense of other elements.

There is plenty of opportunity to do this in other parts of your video or Channel and, if you are consistent enough, that visual style becomes part of the brand.

Phonics Song | Alphabet Song | Alphabet Phonics | Songs For...   The Vowel Song | A E I O U | Phonics for Kids | Phonics Song...   The Letter A Song | Phonics Song | The Letter Song | ESL for Kids |...

YouTube.com/funkidsenglish

2. Make it EYE CATCHING

Yes, I know this is obvious, but there are ways to catch the eye on busy search results pages that are definitely under-used.

In the main, your video will be displayed against a white background, so use borders and white space to create a pattern interrupt and make sure that the eye is drawn to your videos.

Here is a beautiful example of that:

Guessing book plots from the cover design! | with Ariel Bissett

YouTube.com/charlimarietv

3. Use colour to code

There is very little space to convey scheduling on the Channel page nowadays.

However, letting your subscribers know what they can expect, when it is coming and the differences in your types of video are still very important.

If your Channel has multiple strands then a great tip is to use colour as a differentiator between the different types of video.

Yet again you are letting the viewer know exactly what they are getting before they click and anything that works towards this goal is good.

One channel that does an amazing job of using colour is Global Cycling Network - check out their Channel page to see it in full effect at *www. YouTube.com/globalcyclingnetwork*

It is easy to talk about optimized Thumbnails, but the physical production of them takes time, effort and some degree of skill.

If you have the time and ability I would suggest doing this yourself, as you will be in full control of the output.

I personally keep mine simple and clean by using Photoshop.

If you do not have the funds to use a programme like Photoshop, you can find free alternatives such as GIMP or Canva. You can find links all three on my resources page at *www.FAQTube.tv/tools*.

When working with other people's content I have used professional picture editors and the difference in quality from what I can produce is staggering.

If you *do* have the money, the extra investment in professional help could make a huge difference.

If budgets are tight consider a skills-swap or barter with a designer, or if you are lucky you could try and find a reliable designer on *www.fiverr.com* where I have had some success in the past.

This may feel like a big effort for what is seemingly a small part of the YouTube process, but the impact it can have can be gobsmacking.

I have seen the difference a Thumbnail can make.

Go back and review old Thumbnails with a critical eye.

Do they live up to the new standards that you've set for yourself?

If not, go back and re-do them and make sure you track the results in your Analytics.

****

CHAPTER 6 – VIDEO DESCRIPTIONS

A good description can do many things.

Take you to a world you have never been to. Let you see things that do not exist. Tantalise. Tease. And Titillate.

It can also get you more views on YouTube and that is what I am going to help you with in this chapter.

Like any aspect of your YouTube Channel, Video Descriptions have two functions:

◆ To help your content get discovered with solid video SEO

◆ To encourage clicks once it is presented to the audience

But the Video Description has a very powerful third aspect that the other cornerstones of optimization do not.

The ability to link off-platform.

This is a feature that can be hugely important and one that I will go into much more detail shortly.

The optimization of Descriptions was already key but with the recent reduction of the "above-the fold" section, now is the time to make sure that your descriptions are fulfilling their potential.

Steps for optimizing your YouTube Descriptions

. Make it Keyword rich

efore you upload (but ideally before you create) a YouTube video you hould know the exact Keywords and Key Phrases that you want it to ank for in the Search results.

eyword research for YouTube has become increasingly difficult since hey shut down their Keyword tool.

lowever you can carry out basic searches with Google Trends and more dvanced research using paid tools such as Vid IQ, which I use (more at /ww.FAQTube.tv/tools).

)nce you have your Keywords they need to be placed above the fold in he description (viewable by everyone without clicking "Show More") nd they should be reinforced by being included in your Tags and Titles)o.

eep Keywords relevant and honest because, as with Tags, YouTube loes not take kindly to Keyword stuffers or abusers.

ven if you do benefit in the short term from spammy Keyword placement, ou will be hurt in the long run by negative Audience Retention when iewers do not get what they clicked for.

would say a safe bet would be to include individual Keywords twice at nost but make sure they do not seem forced.

Remember you are ultimately writing for humans here, not search engines.

And with that in mind...

2. Sell, Sell, Sell

When composing your Video Title you are hampered by a lack of space in which to sell your video to the audience.

Here is your chance.

Write creatively and work to sell your video to the viewer.

◆ What will they see?

◆ Why should they watch?

◆ How will it benefit them?

Whatever niche you are in, you need to know your audience and what they respond to.

Tease and inform them and make sure to do it in the first 5 lines, as this is all they are guaranteed to see without clicking to reveal more.

This is not a lot of space, but consider yourself lucky as not too long ago this was just two or three lines. You now have more than enough space for a quick synopsis and can drop in a Subscribe link on line five if it tickles your fancy.

3. Include subscription links

Yes, heavy users can get tired of being asked to Subscribe but unfortunately it is just a mechanic of the platform.

You don't have to come across as spammy and instead *suggest* rather than *request* e.g. *"If you found this useful, you can Subscribe here..."*

t is really simple to get a direct link to your subscription opt-in, just add he following to your Channel URL:

sub_confirmation=1

Do not forget to include **http://** before any link you post as this creates an active link, making it clickable for users and visible to YouTube and Google.

4. Link out to websites and other people's videos

No, I have not gone crazy. It IS important to link out to other people's content.

YouTube is a search engine (the second largest in the world in fact) and, like its bigger sibling Google, it uses outgoing links as a ranking factor.

YouTube and Google's main aim (excluding making money) is to provide the most valuable Search results possible to their users.

Linking out to related content helps search engines get a better idea of what your content is about. It also shows that you are interested in helping your viewers.

In terms of linking externally, point to high authority sites such as Wikipedia and notable news and educational sites.

Linking to other videos on YouTube also has a potential advantage where the algorithm may start to associate your video with the video you are linking to. If that video gets lots of views and you start getting presented in the Suggested Videos for it, this will turn into a great source of traffic for you.

Any external linking is a fine balancing act because it could potentially shorten your video Watch Time and the Session Time of the user. I do believe that the benefits far outweigh the potential downside though, as click through rates to these sections are rarely significant.

5. Add links to your own videos and playlists

Click through rates to these sections may be lower than most would like but even if it only generates just a few extra views it is worth the effort.

Point to related videos that viewers would be interested in and, where possible, link to a version that sits in a Playlist.

(Find out how to create a "Playlist Mode" link in my video in the bonus section at *www.FAQTube.tv/bonus*).

That way they are exposed to even more videos and may continue to watch through all of the remaining videos in the Playlist.

This advice goes beyond Descriptions because it is best practice to link in Playlist mode anywhere you link to one of your videos.

6. Make longer content easy to digest

If you are working on longer content why not split it into virtual chapters and link to the time codes in your Description?

You can do this easily by putting the time (mm:ss) in the Description. YouTube then automatically makes it a clickable link to that point in the video.

> **Published on Mar 7, 2014**
> In this video I show you how to use the Google Trends search function to spot what is trending on YouTube so that you can create related content and benefit from the associated traffic.
>
> 1:38 - Learn how to compare two potential keywords
>
> For information on YouTube trends read the full article: http://www.faqtube.tv/trending-on-you...

Anything that gets the audience to stick around, even if they miss a big section of the video, is better than them leaving. This may seem counter-intuitive but giving them the option to skip is in fact a good Audience Retention technique because it is better for them to watch a section of your video as opposed to clicking away and watching none.

he following three tips can be added to your Upload Defaults once, and hen they will automatically be added to any future Description going orward on upload. This is a great time saver and ensures consistency.

lere is how mine look:

For more YouTube help visit http://www.faqtube.tv/

Get your free YouTube optimization ebook here -
http://www.faqtube.tv/youtube-optimization-ebook

Join our race to 1000 YouTube subscribers -
http://www.raceto1k.com

Follow FAQ Tube on Twitter - http://www.twitter.com/faqtube

Like us on Facebook - http://www.facebook.com/faqtube

and come say hello on our G+ page - http://faqtube.tv/gplus

FAQ Tube is the place to come to find out how to do YouTube better.

From opening a YouTube account to advanced YouTube Tutorials this
is place to be if you want more YouTube views, YouTube subscribers
or want to make more money on YouTube.

. Link to your own website

ou do not have one? You should!

f you do, this is useful for traffic generation (make sure you are sending hem to a mobile friendly landing page) and also for the SEO of your vebsite as it is getting a backlink from a high authority domain.

\gain remember point 4 that YouTube (to a certain extent) likes outbound links, especially relevant ones.

8. Link to your Social Media

iome viewers may not be heavy users of YouTube but could be die-hard ans of other social networks.

iive them the option of following you on other platforms if that is what hey want.

I prefer to keep this information quite low in the Description so that it can be found if sought after but so that it does not overshadow more important information or valuable links.

9. Include a description of your Channel

This could be a condensed version of your "About" section and should include the main Keywords for your Channel.

This gives the audience a quick overview of your Channel if they are new and also helps in terms of SEO as YouTube will index this text even though it is "below the fold."

I believe it will also help build a relationship between your videos that will help increase views from Suggested Videos.

Here is a fantastic example of this channel "blurb" from the BBC's Earth Lab Channel:

More about BBC Earth Lab
Welcome to BBC Earth Lab! Always wanted to know What the world's strongest material ? Why trains can't go uphill? Or How big our solar system really is? Well you've come to the right place. Here at BBC Earth Lab we answer all your curious questions about science in the world around you (and further afield too).

As well as our Earth Lab originals we'll also bring you the best science clips from the BBC archive including Forces of Nature with Brian Cox, James May's Things You Need To Know and plenty to keep the Docs away with Trust Me I'm A Doctor.

And if there's a question you have that we haven't yet answered let us know in the comments on any of our videos and it could be answered by one of our Earth Lab experts.

YouTube.com/earthlab

The steps above may seem quite a lot to implement just for your Descriptions, but if you start to use them as a quick five-point checklist (three of them are automated) then this will be a simple part of your upload process that will become second nature.

They will help your overall Channel experience and provide consistency and professionalism as well as helping your wider SEO efforts.

Be sure to put these into action on your next release and go back and change any old Descriptions that no longer live up to your current standards.

F you have lots of videos that you have already published and the nought of going back to update them fills your heart with dread, fear ot there are tools that can help you make bulk updates.

My number one tool for taking care of updating old videos is TubeBuddy. t can update everything from Tags, Descriptions and Titles all the vay through to Cards and End Screens. Find out more by visiting www.FAQTube.TV/tubebuddy

****

CHAPTER 7 - 9 WAYS TO OPTIMIZE YOUR YOUTUBE CHANNEL PAGE

A YouTube Channel Page is a shop window.

It is a chance to sell yourself to new viewers and give them a glimpse of what they can expect should they hit the Subscribe button.

What does your Channel Page say about **your** Channel?

◆ *Is it the best it can be?*

◆ *Is it optimized to highlight your content and convert browsers into Subscribers?*

If you look at the sources of your Subscribers in YouTube Analytics you will probably see that many, if not most, of your Subscribers come from "Channel/Other" and not directly from a video.

This is because after finding a good video, most people check out the Channel Page before subscribing. They do this to make sure the rest of your videos look equally as cool and to see whether or not you are still active and consistent.

With this in mind you need to make your Channel Page an all-singing, all-dancing advertisement for how good your Channel is.

Follow these nine points and it soon will be:

1. Channel Art

I often tell people not to get too hung up on the design elements of their Channel and instead focus on content and its metadata. However, if you have the time or money you may as well go the extra mile and make it look gorgeous.

he latest layout update gives even more real estate to Channel artwork o make sure your artwork takes full advantage.

ou can find the latest Channel Banner image specifications and get free downloadable Photoshop template in the bonus section at ww.FAQTube.tv/bonus

Make sure the Channel Banner conveys the tone and purpose of your hannel and is inviting. You only get one shot at a first impression, emember.

F you can, squeeze in your upload schedule, because anything you can o to get viewers coming back to your Channel is invaluable.

lere are a few standout examples of YouTube Channel art:

YouTube.com/itsokaytobesmart

YouTube.com/vidpow

YouTube.com/earthunplugged

2. Custom Web Links

Custom Web Links give your Channel a look of professionalism and authority and also let people know that you are human (or 'legit', if you are a business Channel).

They also allow you to capture your audience data and turn browsers into fans or followers.

You can edit these links by going to the **About** tab and then hitting the **Pencil Icon** to the right of the word **Links.**

Most Channel managers simply slap in these links without much thought, but I have some tips that will maximize clicks and make these links work harder for you:

I. Include a link to a website you own

Having your own website means that you can collect the details of your audience and own the relationship with them (it currently belongs to YouTube).

It also means that you can take the conversation where you like unrestricted. And, if it is one of your objectives, you can sell them stuff.

Make sure your site has a Favicon – that is the tiny logo that shows on the overlay and in the URL bar of your site. Again it shows a level of professionalism that most sites do not have and is much more eye-catching.

II. Include Social Media links

Even if your only desired outcome is to get people to watch more of your videos and you have no interest in speaking with your audience, you should still be using some form of Social Media.

t is getting harder and harder to appear in people's Subscription Feed, o any chance to get a link or video in front of people should be taken.

f people want to see your videos make it as easy for them as possible. lso make sure any social accounts you link to are appropriate for your udience.

Mixing business with personal on your social accounts is fine but nake sure that anything personal you mention is appropriate (and - pecifically - age appropriate) to your Channel's audience.

f you do play out to a younger audience it may be worth having a eparate account for your personal life.

II. Only link to properties that are actively updated

f you are linking to your external accounts, make sure that they are ctive.

aking people to a website or social account that has not been updated n ages makes you look unprofessional or as though you do not care bout your audience.

ust like you need to keep your Channel updated consistently, you need o persevere with your other accounts to make sure that a fan, follower r potential customer is never left unsatisfied or unhappy.

f you simply cannot keep up with a certain account remove the link ather than send your audience there.

V. Only link to properties that are relevant to your Channel

f you own a website that sells used cars but you have a Beyoncé covers Channel on YouTube, do not connect the two.

his is not relevant to your audience and they may take offence to being aken somewhere that they do not care about. It may result in them not watching any more from your Channel.

V. Make the Link Title stand out (30 characters max)

What is the point of having these links if they do not get clicked?

Give viewers a reason to click with a call to action or a promise of value in return for their visit to the link.

YouTube.com/vidpow

Even though only a small percentage of your traffic will ever come through your Channel Page (and even less come through the About section), it is important that those who do visit get the most professional and satisfying experience possible.

By having these links overlaid you have the chance to take the conversation to a platform of your choice and ultimately to increase engagement with your audience.

Do not forget that if someone likes a video of yours and wants to know more about you, or has already made the choice to follow you off platform as well, do not disappoint them. Make it as easy as possible for them to do this by having an optimized set of links.

The next tip for optimizing your Channel page now.

3. Use up all Sections

A Section is one of the customizable "shelves" that make up the bulk of a Channel Page. I find it hard to understand why some Channels only use a few of their allotted ten Sections. To me, this this is like mailing out a product catalogue with blank pages in it.

Take advantage of the space and fill it with a diverse range of content that shows off what your Channel is all about.

ou can include Sections showcasing Playlists, Liked Videos, Latest Jploads, Most Popular Uploads other Featured Channels and more, so here is no excuse not to fill up the Channel page.

4. Pattern interrupt

f you do use up all of your Sections as recommended in point 3, the page can become a bit of a mess, resulting in a sea of videos and too much choice.

I would recommend mixing up the presentation of Sections between Horizontal Rows and Vertical Lists to create a pattern interrupt.

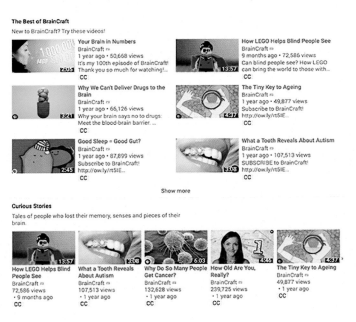

YouTube.com/braincraft

This helps to break up the page into bite-sized chunks and can be used o draw attention to your most valuable Sections.

This option is available directly in the Section Editor:

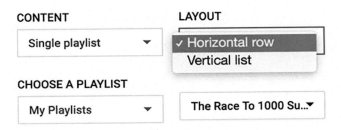

5. Thumbnails

Your Channel page is only going to be as sexy as your Thumbnails, so make sure they are attractive and optimized in order to achieve more clicks and to give a better overall impression of your Channel.

The cure for this is simple – you just need to read chapter 5.

If you have lots of sub-par Thumbnails to go back and optimize them. Start with the videos that appear at the beginning of your Sections and take care of the rest after that.

6. Featured Channels

This feature is easy to overlook, but implementing this simple technique can have massive reputational benefits for your Channel. I see so many people wasting the opportunity that this widget provides when it is so simple to implement - and to implement well.

To see how to enable and set up this widget correctly check out the video in the bonus section - *www.FAQTube.tv/bonus*.

If you have more than one Channel, it makes sense to promote these ahead of other people's Channels, but promoting others can be great for your credibility.

dding other Channels from your category, especially bigger and better nes, creates a subconscious association between your Channel and hose you feature even if there is no link at all.

sychologically there IS a link and you gain credibility by being ssociated with those Channels you feature.

f you are new this also helps the viewer to clarify what your Channel s about because they can use the Featured Channels as a point of eference.

hese are a few of my Featured Channels – all operating in a similar pace to me:

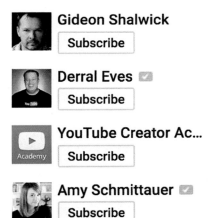

he following points will help you to get the most out of your Featured hannels widget.

. Fill up the widget

here is plenty of real estate here and you may as well use it (ten slots, o be exact).

The more Channels you feature, the more likely the viewer is to recognise another Channel in your space and to then make that all-important association.

If you struggle to fill the widget, it is better to leave slots empty than to add irrelevant or low-authority YouTube Channels.

II. Order them in terms of authority

Like most things on YouTube (see Titles, Descriptions, Playlists) you need to front load the widget so the most important and recognizable Channels appear first.

These are more likely to get noticed, and, if viewers only see one of these in your widget, you want it to be the Channel with the most authority as that is who you would most want to be associated with.

To re-order your widget, simply click the **Pencil Icon** on the widget > **Edit Module** and grab and move the Channel thumbnails by clicking on them in the top left-hand corner:

Added channels

David WalshOnline ☑   Derral Eves ☑   Caleb Wojcik   Nick Nimmin

If you do not want to order them you can also hit the "shuffle" check box so that the order is randomized for the viewer. I use this as I view all of my Featured Channels in equal standing.

III. Tell them you have featured them

One benefit of Featured Channels that we have not discussed yet is the potential relationships that could arise from featuring other Channels in your space.

y featuring other Creators, you are potentially sending them traffic and xposing them to new viewers. Even if you are just starting out, I am ure a Creator or Channel Manager would appreciate this gesture.

each out to them in Video Comments, or on Social Media and let them now you have featured them.

he worst-case scenario is that you get no response.

he best-case scenario is that this leads to an on-going relationship hat could include cross-promotion and collaboration. They may even dd your Channel to their Featured Channels widget.

V. Rename the widget

o not leave the widget named as the default "Featured Channels." This s as dull as ditch water and is much less likely to catch the viewer's eye.

ename it something a little catchier that shows that both you and our Channel have a bit more personality than your average Creator.

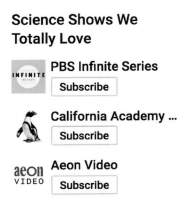

YouTube.com/KQEDDeepLook

his five-minute process can work wonders for your Channel even if it s hard to see a direct effect on views or Subscribers.

This kind of 'soft' optimization will not make your Channel famous overnight, but as part of an optimized Channel Page it will work to cement your reputation as a professional and an authority in your chosen space.

It will also show you to be a genuine paid-up member of the YouTube community. This comes with its own benefits including increased trust and likeability.

Now on to our next fundamental of Channel Page optimization.

7. Unsubscribed Trailer (Channel Trailer)

Undoubtedly this is one of, if not, THE most important elements of your Channel Page.

This video plays automatically when someone who is not yet subscribed visits your Channel and is your best chance to convert them from a browser into a new Subscriber. The Trailer not only needs to show off your best content, but also to reflect what a Subscriber can expect from the Channel.

The worst thing you can do is to not have a custom Trailer at all and just select one of your existing videos instead.

This is not fit for purpose.

And if you do have a Trailer in place already, have you re-watched it recently? Is it the best advert for your Channel today?

Here are my top tips for creating a killer Unsubscribed Trailer.

I. Hook them in early

Don't waste time on branding.

Like any YouTube video, you need an optimized start and nowhere is this more important than in the Unsubscribed Trailer.

ou need to capture them in the first few seconds so front-load it with our most impactful clips. This way viewers know straight away what ind of awesomeness you can deliver.

rom here you can give a broader look at the Channel but keep it tight nd interesting to avoid them clicking away.

would also strip out any branding. This only wastes precious seconds nd, as they are watching on the Channel Page, they are already urrounded by your branding.

(eep it clean and lean and keep them keen.

.. Use the Video Description wisely

;ell the Channel, *not* the video.

Jsually the primary functions of a YouTube Video Description is to sell t to a browser, provide further information and links and to deliver SEO alue in the form of Keywords.

Vhen a video is being used as an Unsubscribed Trailer, this needs to)e adapted so that the description focuses on selling the whole of the :hannel.

This makes more sense when you see the description in the context of he Channel page:

Channel Trailer 2016
5,222 views 1 year ago

Hey there Youtubers, welcome to Tom's Test Kitchen. Here I try to recreate food I have never eaten, maybe it was something I saw on TV or heard about from a friend. Please subscribe to find out what I'm working on next. I usually upload at least two video recipes or a Salsa review each week.

YouTube.com/user/tdjtx

This prime real estate should be used to provide information on what viewers can expect from the Channel. Make your copy as sexy as possible while delivering key information about the videos that Subscribers will get to see if they Subscribe.

Inject it with personality and make sure to SELL the Channel and include a strong call to action to Subscribe. Do not use too many lines to do it though, or it may be cut off, depending on how and where it is being watched.

III. Use a Subscribe call to action throughout

If you have someone on your Channel Page and watching this video you already have him or her hooked.

Your next job is to convert them from browser to a Subscriber.

Nothing will convert better than a strong call to action. I would distribute these throughout the video in relevant places (but do not appear as too desperate) with a bold call to hit the Subscribe button at the end.

When it comes to implementing the call to action, here are my recommendations again in order of effectiveness:

◆ A human, in-vision, giving a verbal call to action and physically pointing where to click

◆ A human in-vision giving a verbal call to action

◆ A voiceover telling people where to click

◆ A Burnt in graphical call to action

IV. Turn off monetization

This *is* an advert. It just happens to be for your Channel.

It is a promotional piece that you want to spread as far and wide as possible and you do not want anything to get in the way of that.

Yes, you may lose out on some small revenues but you will more than make up for that if you have a Trailer that converts better.

Ve are playing the long game here.

Include a schedule

F you are able to set and keep to a schedule then this would be a great lace to illustrate it.

: shows that you are dedicated and consistent and that you have egular features that viewers will not want to miss out on. It also shows hat you offer a fully-fledged Channel experience worth investing time n rather than being a one hit wonder.

'eople are creatures of habit and they crave schedule and routine. Feed he habit.

I. Include "Trailer" in the Title

'his may seem a little pointless but you must remember that this will ot always be seen in the context it was intended – the Channel Page.

'his will be found in Search and Suggested Videos and will appear a ittle strange on its own and out of context.

ty showing clearly that it is a Trailer in the Title it will make more sense o viewers and weed out uninterested browsers who could damage your udience Retention rates.

II. Update/reboot regularly

s time goes by you will be creating more interesting content and weaking longer running series.

Make sure that your Trailer reflects the latest and best versions of your vork as well as your current style and tone of voice.

.ike it or not, as YouTube Channel managers we are also sales clerks nd merchandisers rolled into one.

'his is your Christmas window display.

;how people what you do and show them in style.

Back to our list of Channel Page optimization tips now.

8. Turn on Popular/Recommended Channels

This is the easiest and quickest tip of them all.

If not already activated, go to the right hand sidebar (while logged in) and click **Enable** under **Popular Channels On YouTube**. This will bring up the widget on your YouTube Channel.

Related channels

Enable

Yes, you may be associated with random Channels at times, but the clearer your proposition becomes, the more likely you will be shown against similar quality Channels in your niche.

Not only does this reinforce point 6 but also if you do not turn this on you will not be included in the suggestions on other people's Channels. As you start to grow this could be a good source of traffic that you are missing out on.

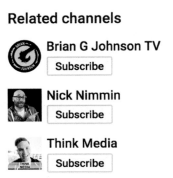

These are all very simple steps to implement. They will make a big impact on the look and feel of your Channel Page.

n optimized Channel Page will work as an advert for your content and how you to be more professional. This in turn will imply your content ; of a higher standard than that of most other Creators. It may not be our biggest source of traffic and Subscribers but it is one that is under our complete control. So make sure you put these suggestions into ractice as soon as possible.

****

CHAPTER 8 – OPTIMIZING AT THE TIME OF UPLOAD

One of the beauties of YouTube is that you can upload a video with just a couple of clicks. It has been designed that way so that anyone and their grandma can be a Creator without any technical knowhow whatsoever.

However, even though it is simple to upload a video, to make sure it is uploaded with all settings optimized is a little more complicated and there are a number of options that can be confusing.

In this chapter I will show you seven tips to make sure you upload and publish your videos so that they are optimized for maximum views.

1. Publish in HD

If a video is in HD, YouTube will put a small flag next to it.

This is because it is important to audiences who want to watch in the best quality possible. It is therefore also important to YouTube, who will take this into account when they have a choice of videos to serve in Search and Suggested.

Today there is very little excuse not to be uploading video in full HD, seeing as the cost of camera equipment has come down so much. Most smartphones also now have the ability to shoot in at least 1080p.

This should be your minimum target as we now have the capability to upload in 60fps, 4k ultra high definition and even 360 immersive

ideo with 3d sound. YouTube is likely to give preferential treatment to
ideos uploaded with the latest specs.

. Select the optimal Category

Vhen publishing or editing a video, on the Advanced Settings tab you
iave the choice of fifteen Categories into which your video should fall.

`hose categories are listed in the image below:

Film & Animation
Autos & Vehicles
Music
Pets & Animals
Sports
Travel & Events
Gaming
People & Blogs
Comedy
Entertainment
News & Politics
✓ Howto & Style
Education
Science & Technology
Nonprofits & Activism

f your video potentially falls into two categories you may choose to go
vith a category that has less competition.

`or example, if you make funny videos about science you may wish to
iut these in the Education category instead of Entertainment which is
i much more common category and is therefore more competitive.

. Optimize Release Time

teleasing consistently is hugely important but equally as important is
inding the perfect time to release in the first place.

The momentum and early success of a video (mainly in the first 24-72 hours) is likely to determine the long-term success of that video.

With this in mind, you should release your videos when your target audience is most likely to be online, so think about where they are in the world (check your Analytics).

Are they likely to be at work? At school? When are they most likely to react to a notification?

These factors should influence your release date and time.

Another benefit of this is that the more your Subscribers see and watch your videos after being notified, the more likely they are to have you as a Recommended Video on their Home screen in the future. The Home screen is particularly important for mobile viewers so this is a really powerful strategy.

4. Go direct to Public

I have heard a lot of discussion about people sending their video Unlisted to certain groups before making it Public.

Do not do this!

Not unless you have a *very* good reason. The same goes for sharing videos as Private before setting them to Public.

This goes hand in hand with point 3 that the first few hours of release are the most important. If it is not available to ALL of your audience once it is technically published then this is going to hurt you.

There has also been much debate about whether or not you should schedule the publication of your videos (if you have this option) as it may break that 72 hour rule.

I disagree with this because I do not believe the clock starts ticking until the video is made Public. Unfortunately I have no scientific evidence of this but I have had a lot of success over the years with videos that have een scheduled and have seen no difference between those and videos nat are set to Public straight away.

cheduling can be a powerful tool if you are running multiple channels r your publishing timetable is based around an audience in a different me zone. For me the benefits of scheduling, especially with working n YouTube at scale, far outweigh the possible downsides.

his is something that you need to consider and experiment with before uilding into your publishing strategy.

. Allow embedding

am not sure why anyone posting their videos publicly would not want nem embedded on sites across the web, but the option is there so I vill discuss it.

Ine reason perhaps might be that if the content is sensitive in nature ou would not want it appearing on certain websites. But I would expect his to be the minority of cases.

llowing the embedding of video has two HUGE benefits:

'iews – If embedded on a site that is getting lots of traffic this can be a ich source of views. I have seen videos receive hundreds of thousands f views by being embedded on a single web page.

EO – YouTube sees that the video is getting lots of views off-platform nd interprets this as the video being particularly good or valuable. It vill then promote this more heavily *on*-platform, leading to even more iews.

o to cut a long story short, ensure this box is checked.

. Allow on non-monetized platforms

Jow this one is not as straight forward to those who are new to the latform and some people may ask:

Why would I want my videos to be played in places where they can't earn money?

And it is a fair question.

The answer lies in the previous point.

Off-platform views send a positive signal to YouTube who then promote the video more on-platform. You then make incremental revenue through these monetized views on YouTube.

Let us break it down, using $1 for each monetized view (we wish!) to illustrate the point in the following two scenarios:

A) Sarah uploads her video and does not allow views on non-monetized platforms. It gets viewed 70,000 times.

70,000 views = $70,000 dollars

B) Sarah checks the box to allow non-monetized playback on her next video.

It gets picked up by a popular lifestyle blog and receives 300,000 views via that embed. YouTube then goes on to promote it internally.

300,000 non monetized views + 120,000 monetized views = $120,000

Although the revenue per view is way down, overall Sarah has made more money, achieved exposure on a relevant blog, and probably picked up a healthy chunk of Subscribers along the way. All by checking one box.

Now, this is not going to be the case on every video but even if it only happens to you once, it is worth it.

7. Closed captions

For all its amazing infrastructure and tech capability, the one thing that YouTube has not nailed yet is "reading" the content of your video.

Ve can fix this by uploading Closed Caption (CC) files to our individual ideos, thereby allowing both YouTube and Google to index every word hat is said in the video.

RODE smartLav vs smartLav+ lavalier mic

YouTube.com/simpleaudiotips

his means you are much more likely to rank for the Keywords included n your script than your competitors who are not transcribing their videos.

he other added bonus of this is that people who are hard of hearing, r people trying to learn English by watching YouTube videos, are much nore likely to choose you over your competition.

)nce you have these Captions in place you could potentially translate hem into other languages. The value of doing this is only going to ncrease as YouTube expands in non-English speaking territories, but nore on that in the next chapter.

low this seems like a lot to do each time you upload but virtually all of t can be set up in your Upload Defaults in your Channel. That way you •nly have to save these settings once and it will apply this as a default o all future uploads.

'ou will need to go and manually change settings for anything that has ılready been published, though.

****

CHAPTER 9 – OPTIMIZING FOR INTERNATIONAL AUDIENCES

Over 70% of views on YouTube come from outside of the US[*] – which is pretty eye opening.

Add to that the fact that it has opened up Creator Spaces in India and Brazil and you get an idea of how much of your audience probably does not speak English as a first language.

Asia and Latin America are two places where growth of the platform is explosive, and there is huge potential for your Channel to grow with it if you know how to attract these international audiences.

Before we look at how we can attract more of them, let me ask; *have you checked where in the world your current subscribers are based?*

You can find out by going to your **Creator Studio > Analytics > Subscribers > ** and then scroll down and hit the **Geography** tab. This will then show your Subscribers' locations.

Source	Geography	Date	Subscription status

Geography	Subscribers* @ ↓
United States	223
United Kingdom	112
India	87

Note that language served is based on the users' Language Settings, NOT their location, but if you have a large audience in a non-English speaking country you can assume many are watching set to their local language.

Confirm the local language with a quick Google Search.

---

[*]   *Source: www.statisticsbrain.com/YouTube-statistics*

. is likely you will see one or two non-English speaking territories/ anguages that make up a decent share of your audience. This shows hat you have appeal in that market and the potential to grow your udience there even more.

will now show you nine ways you can optimize for those international udiences you have picked out.

. *Translate your Captions files*

1 the previous chapter we discussed the benefit of transcribing your ouTube videos and uploading the transcription as a Captions file.)nce you have the Captions files, getting these translated into other anguages greatly increases that benefit.

'his means that not only can foreign-language speakers understand nd engage with a video that they could not engage with previously, but lso that others are more likely to find it because the foreign language aptions will be indexed by YouTube.

ouTube has a few options to help you transcribe your captions if you re not able to do it yourself:

Google Translate is built right into the system – although the reliability of those translations can be somewhat questionable.

I. YouTube have partnered with a number of services that are embedded into the platform that will translate the files for a fee. You will find these on the **Info and Setting page** of your video within the **Translations tab**.

II. You can turn on the setting to allow your audience around the world to translate your Captions for you. The completed Captions are then audited by the community to ensure they are correct before going live.

To enable the Community Contributions on your videos go to **Creator Studio > Translations & Transcriptions**.

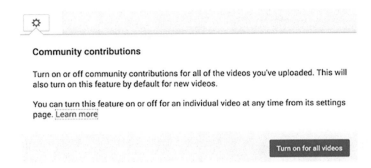

2. *Translate your Titles*

As mentioned previously, YouTube added a new tab to the video Info and Settings Page called "Translations." On this tab you can implement the next three suggestions.

This tab allows you to set metadata in a number of languages so that the text can be indexed and provided to the user based on their Language Settings (not location).

For example, you can set all of your metadata in German so that it is more likely to be served to German-speaking audiences. They are more likely to choose your video over your competitors who do not provide German metadata.

o add a translated Title, go to your video's **Info and Settings** page, hit he **Translations** tab, select your original language from the drop down nd then set the language you are translating into. Now enter your ranslated Title as you would in English.

)o not worry though, your English Title will still be served to everyone lse.

$. Translate your Description

)n the same tab you can also localize the Description into different anguages following the same steps as above.

f you have the language skills, feel free to change the nature of the lescription instead of just doing a straight translation.

)ifferent places and cultures have their own traditions, customs and vays of communicating that are unique to them so try and convey that vhere possible.

)o remember to retain any Keywords you are trying to rank for.

*. Localize links

\nother thing that the Translation tab allows you to do with your)escription is to add unique links that will not appear for other anguages. This can be really powerful because you can send different udiences to different locations.

his is most effective if you have a dual-language website (or landing)ages), are selling products in different stores around the world or if ⁄ou have something available for only one region in the world and you lo not necessarily want to share it with your global audience.

5. Have an optimized release time

If you have two target audiences in very different time zones this can be tricky, but where possible try and find a release time that is optimized for all of your target regions.

This means that potentially you could have the momentum from two audiences driving your video forward in YouTube's algorithm instead of one, leading to many more views overall.

If this is not possible then I would suggest an extra post on Social Media during a time that better suits the viewing habits of your secondary audience.

The next three tips are optimizing for other languages in a big way, and may only work if you speak both languages yourself or if the opportunity for that secondary market is worth the effort and resource:

6. Create bespoke content

All people, no matter where they are in the world appreciate being recognized.

Now, I am not suggesting you have to create dual-language content because that will possibly please no one, but there are things you can do to shout out to your other regional audiences such as:

◆ Including them in competitions/giveaways

◆ Recognizing their national holidays

◆ Giving shout outs to international commenters

◆ Throwing in a cultural reference as an in-joke now and then

YouTube.com/Myvoxsongs

Reply to comments in different languages

you are encouraging people from around the world to watch your ideos, then you should treat them in the same way in the comments s your English speaking audience.

ow, you do not have to have full conversations in other languages but brief acknowledgment of foreign language commenters can go a long vay. It can also encourage repeat comments and others to follow suit.

Double-Up branding / free text

or this to work you would probably need an audience split of about 0/50 in two target languages because otherwise it could be seen to e a bit over the top.

mplementing this is quite simple, but quite bold.

Here you would replicate any free text you had on the Channel (excluding itles, Tags, and Video Descriptions) in your two main languages.

or example:

▶ Any text in your Channel Banner

▶ Any text in your Channel Icon (avatar)

▶ Your Channel Description from your About section

▶ Your Playlist descriptions

It would be best if your audiences are aware that you have a big following in two distinct places in the world so they are not confused when they see the dual branding.

9. Be mobile friendly

In many parts of the world where YouTube is seeing the fastest growth, the quality of Internet and its speed and infrastructure are not great, and the majority of traffic comes via mobile networks and devices.

So for audiences in growing markets like Brazil and India (where YouTube has recently launched a mobile app to compensate for poor internet speed) it is even more important to be optimized for viewers on mobile.

To find out the best ways in which you can do this, check out the next chapter.

****

CHAPTER 10 – OPTIMIZING FOR MOBILE VIEWS

ouTube has stated publicly that mobile views make up about 50% of ll Watch Time on the platform (more than that is some territories). hat is a whopping 25% increase since they last updated the statistic.

would be surprised if, by the time you read this that number is not loser to 60%.

Have you seen this trend in your **Analytics**? Check by clicking **Creator itudio > Analytics > Devices**:

Device type @	Watch time @ ↓ (minutes)
Computer @	73,159 (73%)
Mobile phone @	20,162 (20%)
Tablet	6,574 (6.5%)
TV @	382 (0.4%)
Game console @	256 (0.3%)

:ven if it is not your reality now, it will be soon, so follow these six steps o optimize for mobile views and viewers. Make sure that you are not osing out because you have overlooked the mobile audience:

!. Embrace '2nd Generation' Annotations

"hese newer types of Annotation work seamlessly across all devices. "he fact that "traditional" Annotations did not work on mobile is the eason they were decommissioned recently.

"hese new Annotations include:

:ards – These can be found on the video's Edit screen, just look for the I" Icon.

Info & Settings   Enhancements   Audio   End screen & Annotations   ⓘ Cards   Subtitles/CC

These should be your go-to widget to replace traditional Annotations.

A Card is a discreet, onscreen marker present throughout the video, but it can also pop out with a small teaser alert at a point you can program

Like traditional Annotations, you can point to a video or Playlist, an associated website, a Channel Page or (unique to Cards) hold a poll that your audience can vote on.

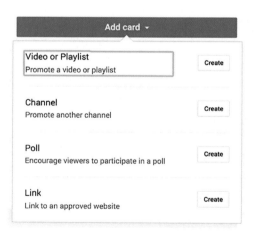

Featured Content - formerly known as In-Video Programming, this creates a pop out alert with video Thumbnail, Title and free text across all of your videos.

You can choose the video or Playlist to promote and then choose the time at which this pops out. The alert can be programmed to appear either at the end of your videos or at a custom start time. A checkbox will also give you the option to let YouTube optimize the timing of this appearance based on previous audience behaviour.

I would suggest never having this pop up at the start of your videos, as this will certainly affect your Audience Retention statistics.

You can set all of this up in your **Creator Studio > Channel > Featured Content** and then by selecting your **featured video and other custom options**.

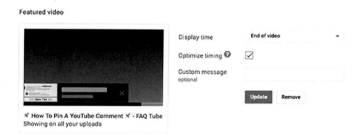

Please note that this Featured Content widget will not display on videos where you already have Cards enabled. I still recommend using this however, especially if you have a lot of older videos that do not carry Cards.

Branding Watermarks - This is the small image overlay that you can set to appear on all of your videos, that when clicked, becomes a Subscribe button.

Branding watermark

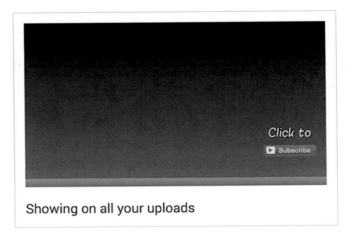

Showing on all your uploads

These are a quite subtle and can be left running throughout the entire video without causing anyone too much annoyance.

It also gives the viewer the chance to Subscribe to you with one click or touch throughout the entire length of the video. This is why I can't recommend it highly enough.

The specifications of this image should be as follows:

◆ PNG or GIF format

◆ Max file size of 1mb

◆ Transparent

And my top tip for this is (no matter how you choose to brand this) to include the word "Subscribe" somewhere in the image somewhere. Otherwise it is not clear to new users that this is a button at all.

And finally and most exciting for me is the latest edition to the Annotation family...

End Screens – These are amazing because they replace the need for you to make complicated "burned in" calls to action and video previews. Instead they allow you to have a fully customizable and more importantly, clickable, set of options for your audience at the end of each video.

These end screens can be up to 20 seconds long and can be made up of up to four different elements. The elements you have to choose from are:

◆ Video or Playlist

◆ Subscribe

◆ Channel

◆ Link

One thing to note is that at least one of these elements MUST be a video. This is not a big deal as you should always be pushing someone to more video where possible anyway.

To make these as effective as possible, I would suggest you interact with these elements directly in video as you are much more likely to get viewers to take action. Here is a perfect example from Derral Eves:

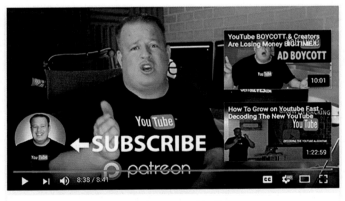

Super Easy Way View Analytics on Any YouTube Video

YouTube.com/derraleves

If this is not possible though you can get a free Photoshop template to help you create a graphical End Screen template inside the bonus section at *www.FAQTube.tv/bonus*.

2. Optimized Thumbnails

These will be even smaller on mobile devices than they are on desktop so make sure they are clean, clear and contrasting.

YouTube.com/carthrottle

Follow my guide to Thumbnails as laid out in chapter 5, paying even more attention to how legible text is.

3. Optimized Titles

As I pointed out in in chapter three it is important to have the "Hook" of your video at the start of the Title, including any Keywords or Key Phrases you want your videos to rank for.

YouTube.com/asweetpeachef

With even fewer characters from your Title shown on mobile devices there is even more reason to frontload them.

4. Graphics must be clear

ny use of on-screen graphics must be clear and sharp. This is especially mportant if you are using burned in subtitles.

Choose a contrasting colour from the main video so that any text or mages are still visible at a smaller size. Where possible, reinforce the raphics with verbal cues just in case.

Leo vs STR 1 v 1 goals challenge - Day 14 of 90

YouTube.com/STRskillSchool

peaking of verbal...

5. Good audio quality

iome people - myself included - believe that good audio is as important, f not more important, than visuals when it comes to online video.

Many viewers can cope with something that is not full HD but if they annot make out what you are saying they are going to jump ship.

Nowhere is that more important than on mobile devices, which often ave weak and tinny audio outputs or are used with cheap headphones.

Make the extra effort to deliver quality audio. It does not have to reak the bank either – there are a number of affordable microphones on the market that give excellent sound. Check out the ones I use at *www.FAQTube.tv/tools*.

6. Make sure your blog/website is responsive

If you send mobile viewers to a site you own and it is not responsive when they get there (i.e. it does not adjust to display nicely on all screen sizes), then they are going to have a horrible experience.

If this is the case they are likely to leave before they get a chance to look around, let alone join your mailing list or buy your product.

Make sure your site is mobile ready by using a responsive theme or have a developer look at it if it has been custom built.

Mobile usage is only going to grow, so take steps now before you start to alienate a HUGE part of your audience (and potential audience).

****

THE FINAL WORD ON YOUTUBE OPTIMIZATION

1y final piece of advice is to stay squeaky clean in terms of metadata nd stay on YouTube and Google's good side.

o NOT mislead your audience.

lo short-term gain will beat the long-term success that optimized and ccurate metadata can bring.

ou should be spending just as much effort optimizing your content for ouTube as you do creating videos, if not more.

fter all, what is the point of epic content if no one is watching it?

tart by building these tactics into your everyday Channel management rocesses, and before you know it you will be optimizing your videos ithout even thinking about it.

ou do not need to take my word for it when it comes to these strategies. mplement them and track them in your Analytics, paying close attention your Traffic Sources, and views from Search and Suggested Videos pecifically.

ouTube is a platform that changes dramatically and quickly. The uttons you need to press and what new features are available are onstantly evolving with every month that passes.

1ake sure you are always up to date by joining the FAQ Tube online ommunity by visiting the bonus section where you will also find all f the videos, bonus articles and worksheets mentioned earlier in the ook.

ww.FAQTube.tv/bonus

1y final word on optimization is that no matter how much the platform hanges, the foundations of what makes videos get watched and shared emain the same.

Follow the strategies in this book and you will be safe in the knowledge that your Channel is being run like a professional. Your videos will be working harder for you and ultimately you will be getting the results you want on YouTube.

The results your videos deserve.

I hope you found this book useful and if you did I would appreciate it if you would consider leaving a review on Amazon.

I would love to get your feedback and these reviews will also help other fellow Creators to discover the book.

*****

ABOUT THE AUTHOR

Tom Martin is Certified by YouTube as an expert in Audience Growth and Digital Rights. He has worked with successful YouTube Creators and Fortune 500 companies to improve their results on YouTube, specializing in both YouTube optimization and YouTube channel strategy. He has dedicated his time to make sure that all of his knowledge and experience is available to his audience so they can improve their YouTube results too.

Tom ran the YouTube channels for BBC Worldwide for over 4 years, dramatically growing their views, subscribers and revenues. Highlights from this time include launching the official YouTube channels for both Sherlock and Doctor Who and taking the Top Gear YouTube channel from 750,000 subscribers to over 3,000,000 in just 12 months. He has spoken at events such as VidCon and written about YouTube for esteemed publications such as Social Media Examiner as well as being a guest on the industry's biggest Podcasts.

To learn more about Tom go to: *www.FAQTube.tv/about*

Made in the USA
Monee, IL
01 December 2020